Still Standing
My Journey from Pain to Purpose

KERRI LeDOUX

Still Standing
My Journey from Pain to Purpose

KERRI LEDOUX

ENCORE
DIRECT TO PRINT

© 2018 by Kerri LeDoux. All rights reserved.

Published by Encore Direct to Print, PO Box 427, Enumclaw, WA 98022

Redemption Press is honored to present this title in partnership with the author. The views expressed or implied in this work are those of the author. Redemption Press provides our imprint seal representing design excellence, creative content, and high quality production.

Scripture quotations are taken from the Holy Bible, New Living Translation, copyright ©1996, 2004, 2015 by Tyndale House Foundation. Used by permission of Tyndale House Publishers, Inc., Carol Stream, Illinois 60188. All rights reserved.

No part of this publication may be reproduced, stored in a retrieval system, or transmitted in any way by any means—electronic, mechanical, photocopy, recording, or otherwise—without the prior permission of the copyright holder, except as provided by USA copyright law.

Cover Photo Leigh Ann Thompson Photography

ISBN 13: 978-1-68314-716-9
        978-1-68314-717-6 (ePub)
        978-1-68314-718-3 (Mobi)

Library of Congress Catalog Card Number: 2018945665

Dedication

This book is dedicated in loving memory to my precious son,
JOHN LEONARD CALLAN,
a servant leader whose time on earth was cut too short
but whose legacy and impact will be remembered forever.
The joy and inspiration he shared with others was infectious.
I'll see you in heaven, Sweet Boy.

*"Sometimes
life is like a glow stick.
You have to be broken
in order to shine."
-Unknown*

Introduction

People say God won't give us more than we can handle, but sometimes life throws us too many curve balls at one time. Responsibilities, burdens, commitments and tragedies get stacked on top of each other until we fear our whole world may come tumbling down. Where is God in those moments? How do we hang on to hope when we are under the crushing weight of loss, anxiety, and stress?

That is the place I found myself in November 2016 when my seventeen-year-old son, Johnny, was tragically killed in a single-car accident on his way to a livestock show. When I was first told about his death, I couldn't—*wouldn't*—believe it was true. I fell to the floor screaming, "Why?" and lived for months in a fog, unable to process the smallest of decisions ...

... until I saw my son in a dream and was reassured he is happy in heaven. That is when God interrupted the trajectory of my thoughts and showed me a new way of life filled with hope and gratitude.

How did God help me heal and give me the strength to go on? When and how did God intervene and plant a new passion and purpose in me to bless others and honor my son's life? How can you, by faith, come to believe God wants to do the same for you? What desire does God want to birth in you today?

I hope you will find answers to those questions and more as you read this book. It is the story of my life, my dreams, my heartbreaking losses, and the powerful way God walked with me through it all and led me to a place I never imagined I would be.

The pain of loss never goes away. It takes a toll on the entire family. But I clung to the comfort Scripture offers in Romans 8:28 –"For we know that God works all things together for good for those who love him and are called according to his purpose." His purposes are so much bigger than we can fathom.

God turns darkness into light. He shines through the smallest flicker of faith and guides us through our grief with a gentle heart of compassion and love. I pray that my story encourages and inspires you to dream beyond your grief. Don't deny your pain and sadness. Give yourself permission to grieve at your own pace while you trust in God's promise of a wonderful plan and purpose for you on the other side.

As I drew closer to God through my grief, I learned to rely more and more on my faith in Jesus and His love for me and my family. After months of mourning, I came to understand that God did not take my son. He received what was His all along and welcomed him to his eternal home.

Proverbs 3:5–6 says, "Trust in the Lord with all your heart, and lean not on your own understanding; in all your ways acknowledge him, and he shall direct your paths."

May you be richly blessed through my story, and may the God of all hope fill you with peace and joy as you seek Him. God has a wonderful plan for your life. I would love to hear your story as it unfolds.

Much love,

Kerri

One

Learn to Live with Loss

You Are Not Alone

"God blesses those who mourn,
for they will be comforted."
~ *Matthew 5:4*

It was 5:20 a.m. Though darkness covered the room, the forecast was calling for another warm sunny day. A perfect day for our long drive home.

Everyone was asleep at my in-law's cozy farmhouse. My husband and I and two of our children had driven close to 500 miles, from our home in Jacksboro, Texas, to Louisiana to spend a few days with his family at Thanksgiving.

My son, Johnny, asked to stay with his grandparents in Texas so he could participate in the Fall Classic in Waco—one of the largest jackpot shows. The Fall Classic is an event where kids go to compete for awards on various species of animals like goats, pigs, sheep, etc. Johnny had a goat that he loved. He affectionately named him Ron Burgundy, and he really enjoyed entering Ron in various goat competitions.

Though his text woke me from a deep sleep, I smiled. I knew it was Johnny. He and Ron were leaving early for the show. We had talked the night before, joking and laughing about upcoming holidays and discussing Christmas gift ideas. He promised to drive safely, and he ended his text with "I love you."

Little did I know it would be the last text I would ever receive from him.

My husband, Gus, and I enjoy playing practical jokes on each other. He's much better at it than I am, but it's always been a playful part of our relationship. I couldn't imagine why he would think it would be funny to joke about my son being killed in a car accident. Yet that's what I thought when he came into the room as I was preparing to head home with him and the kids.

"Kerri, I don't know how to tell you this," he said.

I could barely hear his voice as he mumbled the words, his face contorted in a way I'd never seen before. When our eyes met, I knew something was terribly wrong but I never imagined just how traumatic that something would be.

As he continued to speak, my mind went blank. I heard him say, "Johnny was in an accident. He didn't survive," but I couldn't seem to grasp what he was saying. My knees buckled as my body went limp in his arms.

Then I cried and screamed: "Why? Why? Why? What am I supposed to do now?"

My mother-in-law ran up the stairs, took me in her arms, and tried to comfort me, saying, "I don't know, but we have the same heart."

She understood only too well what I was feeling, because she had lost a son when he was twenty. At that moment, I realized I had become a member of a group I never wanted to be part of.

My daughter, Alexis, heard my screams and ran to find out why I was so upset. When Gus told her, she sobbed in his arms while my mother-in-law continued to hold and comfort me.

Soon after, we packed the truck to go home. It was the longest eight-hour ride of my life. Gus drove fast, like we were in a hurry to get home, but why? Johnny was already gone.

Opening the door to our house, the first thing I saw were my son's shoes. I carried them to his room, laid them next to his bed, and quietly shut the door as though I could erase the painful truth and bring him back to life.

As I walked to the kitchen, family members started to arrive, each one in shock, not knowing what to say. I felt like they were watching my every move, waiting for me to break down in front of them. Several minutes later, I realized the pressure inside me could no longer be contained. I felt like I was going to burst. So I slipped out the door, sat on the ground, and wept.

My mom came outside and held me, followed by my brother. When I told them I felt pressure to entertain the people in my home, they went inside and asked everyone to go to my mother's house to give me some time to grieve. With everyone gone, I finally felt free to climb into bed and just "be".

I could cry out to God, stare at the wall, or sleep—whatever I felt I needed to do—without an audience. I wanted to lay there forever, lost in my pain, but Johnny's school had planned a candlelight vigil the next night to honor him, and I knew I needed to be there.

Words were spoken. Songs were shared. But I couldn't tell you what was said or sung. I just sat in the gym in an emotional fog waiting to be escorted out before anyone else was released. I couldn't bear to talk to anyone that night. Yet, in the midst of my pain, I could feel Jesus's presence with me. His comfort laying over me like a warm blanket of calm. His promises leading me slowly toward His peace that passes all understanding.

On the morning of the viewing, I found a box in Johnny's closet and pulled it out to take to the funeral home. It contained letters Johnny had written, awards he had won, and items he had made with his own two hands. His favorite song was even included in the collection. It was like he was planning his own funeral.

Though I had been advised not to look at his broken and bruised body before it was prepared for his casket, I knew I had to. I was desperate for closure. I was his mother, and I needed to connect with my son one last time.

As others gasped and cried out seeing my son's body and the trauma he had suffered, I stood silently waiting, preparing my heart for the reality I was about to face. After a few moments, I raised my hand to his and gently touched it. His hand was cold and clammy like it always felt, but there was a stiffness now, an ever-present emptiness. Then I asked everyone to please leave the room so I could have a moment alone with him.

I sat in a chair near the table where he was lying, and I prayed before I slowly lifted the covers to see what his body had been through. In that moment I felt the pain of his broken bones penetrate my body. My heart broke into a million pieces. The thought of him suffering was almost more than I could bear.

Making funeral plans with my husband, preacher, parents, and Johnny's biological father was just as heart-wrenching. No one wants to talk about, or even think about, having to plan their child's funeral. As Eugene, our preacher, tried to comfort me in the midst of my pain, the following words sprang from my mouth: "Johnny was never my son to lose. He was God's child. I just had the privilege of raising him."

Eugene stood weeping as he replied, "Most people don't understand that."

I was as astonished as he was when I spoke those poignant words, but now I see that Jesus was speaking through me—through my pain. The Bible says He is acquainted with sorrow, not just any sorrow, but *our* sorrow. He feels our pain and bears it with us.

Our family before the accident

It's always more comforting to talk with someone you relate to who you believe knows exactly how you feel and what you are walking through. Jesus is the ultimate comforter. I know that from personal experience, but that didn't change the fact that I had to walk through the grief.

Although I didn't feel like attending the formal viewing, I knew that the people who cared about my son needed to see me there. They needed closure too, after all, and an opportunity to express their condolences.

I stood outside for two hours as people waited to hug me and confirm to me how very special my son was. I felt blessed and proud to have raised a son who impacted so many in such meaningful ways. Still in shock, I didn't cry at the viewing, but the tears were ever-present, ready to spill out when I least expected it.

Johnny was young, so the funeral director scoured social media to get an estimate of how many people might attend the funeral in order to be well prepared. The amount of posts was so significant that they asked if it would be okay to hold the funeral in the high school gym, advising it was the only place big enough to hold everyone.

As it turned out, they were right. More than 1,500 people were present that day, though I never glanced at their faces. I walked in staring at the floor, knowing if I made eye contact with anyone and saw the sadness on their faces, I would lose my battle to contain my tears. My husband literally held me up as I walked because my knees were so weak.

Johnny's funeral in the high school gym

While I don't remember the details, I do remember feeling that the funeral was beautiful. A perfect way to memorialize my sweet son.

In the days that followed the accident, I felt like I had to know everything my son went through before he died. I visited the crash site and visualized each tragic moment. Pieces of Johnny's truck were scattered everywhere, along with debit cards and personal items. Shavings from his goat, his goat's collar—even his goat, Ron Burgundy, who also died in the accident.

Johnny with Ron Burgundy

I'll never forget my daughter saying she was glad Ron Burgundy died too. When I asked why, she said because then Ron and Johnny could be together in heaven. I had not thought of it that way, but was deeply touched by my daughter's compassionate comment.

I went to see Johnny's truck and called the highway patrolman who was there to ask him every question I was anxious to know the answer to. A friend of mine called and told me her husband had gone to the scene of the accident and met the man who found Johnny. Apparently, the man walked over to my friend's husband and said he wanted to know about the boy's family. The man's name was John.

Immediately, I wanted to see him. Talk to him. Ask him everything about what he had witnessed that morning. Thankfully, when I phoned, he agreed to meet me, and he graciously answered many of the questions I had. Some, however, he refused to answer, which made me angry. Only when he shared that he had a son die the same way at the same age did I feel that, perhaps, he was protecting my mother's heart by keeping some answers to himself.

A month later, as my husband and I sat at church on Christmas morning, our preacher began to call people forward for prayer. He started with, "If you need prayer, come forward."

Gus and I didn't move, so he said, "If something has happened in your life lately that is unimaginable, come forward and let us pray for you." We remained seated as our preacher became more emphatic with his invitation to prayer.

Finally, I looked at Gus and said, "He's talking to us. If we don't get up, he is fixing to say our names." At that, we stood and walked forward for prayer. In the end, what touched me the most was seeing the entire congregation standing and praying over us when we turned around to return to our seats. It was a powerful confirmation of their incredible love for us and support for our family.

With the accident still fresh in my mind, I continued to struggle for weeks, until the night Johnny appeared in a dream. I saw him kneeling down in front of me and, with great enthusiasm, telling me that God is real and heaven is amazing. He also told me that he was lifted above the accident, that he watched the entire crash unfold. And then he was gone.

It was a short, sweet, comforting message that God allowed me to receive in order to help me take another step forward in my healing process.

Grief can cripple you. It makes you feel isolated, alone, damaged, and scared. When people tell you to move on before you're ready to move on, the opposite happens. The pain intensifies and you begin to hide your feelings to avoid other people's comments and concern.

I don't know your story, but I do know that loss is loss. Whether you've lost a dream, a child, a relationship, or anything else significant to you, it hurts. Your pain is valid, and grieving is necessary if you want to be emotionally healthy again.

Please know you are not alone in your pain. God is with you. Even if you're angry with Him, He will never leave you. He is not uncomfortable with your sadness. He will see you through. You will find joy again and be led to a new—or renewed—passion and purpose if you believe in the one who can bring good from every failure, wound, and loss.

My story is a testimony of that. I pray you will invite God to do the same for you.

Two

Put the Past in Its Place

Mistakes Become Masterpieces in God's Hands

"Let all that I am praise the LORD…
He forgives all my sins…
He fills my life with good things."
~ Psalm 103:2–5

I am not the product of a perfect family, though I dreamed that one day I would be the wife and mother of one. My parents are the most amazing people, but both came from broken marriages. My mother had four children before she married my dad and had me.

Sometimes I felt as if I was an only child, because my half-siblings seemed to relate to one another better than to me. I felt rejected because I had a dad and they didn't, and I believed they resented me for that. Their biological dad had been killed in a car accident when my youngest half-brother was six months old. The devastating feeling of not being included in my own family caused me to develop deep insecurity and low self-esteem.

When I was in the third grade, my best friend and I had identical jackets. We wore them everywhere we went. One day at school, I saw her rip a hole in her jacket when she caught it on a pole on the playground. As it got warmer outside, a lot of the kids in our class tossed their coats onto a big pile on the ground and continued to play.

Dad holding me, mom, and my four half-brothers and sisters

My friend said, "Hey, let's throw our jackets on there, too." So, we did.

When recess ended, she beat me to the pile and grabbed one jacket while I grabbed the other. I soon noticed the hole in the jacket I grabbed and told her she had my jacket, but she denied it and wouldn't give it back.

I went home in tears because I was too scared to stand up for myself. I was more afraid of losing her friendship than I was of losing my jacket. My mom ended up going to the school to get it back, but it didn't help me feel much better.

At that young age I already felt like I was at the bottom of the rung. Insecure. Timid. Weak. But I didn't understand why, or how it would affect the rest of my life.

In junior high I had a crush on a boy, and everyone knew it. He was a year older, tall, and blond. Best of all, he seemed to be more of an introvert, quiet like me. One day a group of popular kids told me if I asked him out, he would say yes. I don't know why I believed them, but I did. I summoned what little courage I had, walked up to him, and asked him out while everyone watched. When he said no, they all started to laugh. But all I wanted to do was cry. I was humiliated and heartbroken at the same time, and I vowed that day to never ask a boy out again.

Fortunately, I wasn't completely without talent and friendship. I played basketball on the A-team through junior high and thought I was pretty good. Each year I looked forward to basketball season when I would be part of the team and feel like I fit in at school. It was the one area I was confident I excelled in, and I was desperate to know my parents were proud of me.

Me in my junior high A-team uniform

Unfortunately, when I entered high school, all of my friends made the A-team, but I did not. Suddenly, I didn't feel like I was good enough at anything. I wasn't sure I even wanted to try. That's when I dropped out of sports and began to hang out with kids who were not the best influence on me. I started going to parties and drinking. I felt compelled to do things that just made me feel worse, but also made me feel like I was part of a group again, like I fit in.

I did date someone I thought was a nice boy for a while, but when we broke up, he took all of the pictures he had of me and wrote hurtful words on them. Then he hung them up on every order menu at the local Sonic. Once again, I felt completely humiliated and wanted to run away and hide.

I felt so lost and alone. Hanging out with my friends wasn't even fun anymore. Mean girls seemed to love intimidating the insecure timid kids. Once, a girl who was a total bully rolled her car window down as she was driving through town, stuck her head out of the window, and started screaming bad names at me. I was terrified she was planning to beat me up, and I didn't even know what I had done to make her hate me so much.

Fear and insecurity had a strong hold on me. Bad decisions seemed to be the ones I made more often than not. While still in high school, I started dating a guy who was four years older than me just because he seemed to be interested in me, and I desperately needed attention and affection.

It would be one of the worst decisions of my life. I was young and stupid and I thought I knew it all, but he ended up beating me just because I was late to a rodeo. When he was done with me, I could barely see out of my eyes because they were so swollen and scratched.

My quest for love and acceptance would continue after graduation into future relationships. No matter what went right in the beginning, it seemed almost inevitable the relationship would eventually unravel. Somehow I always felt like I alone had failed. Even after I married and experienced the miracle of becoming a mom, the devious devils of heartache and loneliness returned when we divorced and I became a young single mother of two small children.

Because I worked all day, I had a hard time staying home with the kids every night. After I tucked them in bed, I would sit around the house and feel sorry for myself. The loneliness hurt so much and reminded me of my years growing up, feeling like I didn't fit in. Here I was, a single mom with two young children, struggling with self-doubt, trying to find pleasure and joy in the midst of insecurity. As I had in my younger years, I allowed rejection to creep into my soul and lead me in the wrong direction.

Some girlfriends noticed I was struggling, and they invited me to go out with them. We were having a great time, with guys buying us drinks all night. At one point in the evening, a guy bought me a drink, and after I drank it, my mind went blank. I don't remember anything that happened the rest of that night. That experience scared me enough to pay more attention to who I was around. I had kids to take care of, and being a good mom meant a lot to me.

I could go on and on sharing the many mistakes and poor choices I made in my past; some that are so painful and complicated they are difficult to talk about. Thankfully, despite myself and my own failings, God helped me accept my past and move forward, rather than dwell on my guilt and shame.

I am so grateful that I am not alone in my loss or my sin. Romans 3:23 says that all have sinned and fallen short of the glory of God. Some of us just take a longer road to redemption than others.

The most painful part of failure is the way some people can use our weakness and failure to shame and humiliate us, which can easily drive us toward isolation from God and others. Sometimes the shame feels so overwhelming we can no longer discern who the "good guys" are. We lose our way and our ability to trust anyone, even the closest of friends.

I used to be very sensitive to the opinions of others, but now I realize that my sensitivity stemmed partly from my own wounded heart. I had not forgiven myself for my many mistakes. I was trying to hide from them and pretend the shame and guilt no longer had a hold on me. But when others threw my failures in my face, I reverted to the humiliated little girl at school who felt rejected and unworthy.

Over the years, I heard at church that some of the greatest men and women in the Bible failed, and God healed, forgave, and restored them to places of authority and great blessing. As my heart continued to heal, I began to grasp the truth of God's grace. Why wouldn't He do the same for me? I knew He loved me.

The day God freed and forgave me was the day I was with my mom and dad at the hospital as my dad was suffering with congestive heart failure. I called my preacher, Eugene, at 1:30 in the morning to ask for prayer over the phone, but he hung up and drove to the hospital instead. As Dad gasped for air, Eugene prayed over him beside his bed, then he walked closer to where my mom and I were and sat down.

I'm not sure how the conversation began. All I remember is confessing my sins to Eugene and giving him authority to pray over me. I didn't realize how much guilt and shame I was still carrying inside. I had tried to convince myself I was okay, but I was wrong. His prayer for my forgiveness, healing, and blessing poured into my heart and soul early that morning; and when he left, I was filled with peace. I knew at that moment I was finally free.

As the Word of God says in 1 John 1:9, "If we confess our sins, he is faithful and just to forgive us our sins and to cleanse us from all unrighteousness." Boy, did I learn that truth in my dad's hospital room that day.

God has shown me so much about His love and grace since that morning. He has built within me a confidence in His power and strength that I no longer fear failure like I once did. Now I know that failures can be very good if we learn from them and allow them to inspire us.

Every mistake we make teaches us something about ourselves, about who we are, what our limits and capabilities might be, and what we can and cannot do. They help us live with greater compassion and tolerance for ourselves and others.

The greatest lesson of all that I learned about failure is that God is anxious to forgive us and give us a second chance. If we simply confess our sins, He promises He will forgive us. And we need to learn how to forgive ourselves and no longer carry the weight of our mistakes with us.

No one is perfect, though some people may try to convince us otherwise. We actually perform best when we strive to accomplish goals with excellence, not perfection. Who wants to be perfect anyway? Perfection leaves no room for improvement.

In the event you make a mistake so big that God is the only one you have to lean on, trust Him to carry that burden for you. Every mistake I made, and the consequences I paid as a result of those mistakes, eventually strengthened my faith and drew me into a deeper relationship with God.

Don't quit. Don't hide in guilt or shame or rejection or fear. You have a reason to keep going. You are not your mistakes. Mistakes are what you make. They do not define who you are. You may fail, but you are never a failure.

Pursue a closer relationship with God. Depend on His strength to see you through. Don't focus on the things of this world. Believe, by faith, that God has an amazing plan for your life.

Praise God for every blessing. Pray often and wait for Him to inspire your thoughts. I promise He will lead you to His specific purpose for your life, just as He is leading me.

Three

Believe in the Goodness of God

Powerful Bonds Are Built through Pain

"O Lord, you are so good,
so ready to forgive,
so full of unfailing love
for all who ask for your help."
~ Psalm 86:5

When I was a little girl in my small town of Jacksboro, my heart was filled with little girl dreams. More than anything I wanted to be a wife and mother, to hold and nurture little ones as they grew, and to have someone to love and be loved by.

I suppose that's why, at the age of eighteen, I married a man I met at a party a few months after high school graduation. We dated only six months before becoming husband and wife. I fell hard for him and believed we would spend the rest of our lives together.

Anxious to be a mom, I told him early in the marriage that I was ready to start a family. Unfortunately, he was not. He tried to talk me into buying a new car instead, assuming that would fill the emptiness inside me and buy him a little more time. When I persisted with my desire, he gave in, and within a few short months, I was pregnant. At twenty-two years of age, I gave birth to a beautiful little boy whom we named Johnny.

The first time I held my sweet Johnny

I was in heaven. Touching the palm of his tiny hand as he wrapped his fingers around mine was love to me. For the first time in my life, I felt like I understood what pure happiness was. Johnny instantly captured a special place in my heart. Two years later, when I gave birth to our daughter, Alexis, I felt like our family was complete. My dream of becoming a mother was fulfilled, and my children became the center of my world.

It didn't take long, however, to realize the toll motherhood can take when the mom works full time in addition to having little ones at home. I worked all day, picked the kids up from their babysitter, cooked dinner, bathed the kids and put them to bed, cleaned the kitchen, collected and organized stray toys and other items, laid out tiny outfits for the next day, and finally took time for a bath to unwind myself.

As millions of women know, after all of that, a husband wants—and deserves—some time and attention, but I found it too difficult to give. I was exhausted after using all of my time and energy to care for everything and everyone else all day. I truly felt like I had nothing left to give him at night.

The shock of shifting from best friends to enemies seemed to happen overnight, but I realize now that it began to happen when Johnny was little, and it reached its peak when Johnny was three and Alexis was one. That was the year Joe and I divorced.

We married young and had a lot of fun, but once the children were born, I yearned to be home while he preferred to travel the world. One day at a time we simply grew apart until we no longer wanted to be together.

Fortunately, we had a civil divorce and continued to be friends. While numerous decisions regarding the kids sometimes caused turmoil, we always tried to focus on what was best for them, hoping it would help them through their own healing.

We did not take divorce lightly and even talked about trying to get back together throughout the first year we were apart. We questioned if we had made a mistake. Were we really done? One night when Joe dropped the kids off, we both realized we still loved each other and wondered if we should try again.

It was agonizing to try to figure out the right and best thing to do for everyone involved. At the time, it helped me to look at our divorce as an opportunity to start fresh, to rebuild my life as a single mom despite the pain and frustration of being alone.

Focusing on my children, I found renewed joy in watching them discover new things and learn new talents. Despite my physical exhaustion, one giggle, smile, or hug from either one of them would rejuvenate me and fill me with just enough energy to survive another day. I can honestly say that through all of the trials and tribulations of being a single parent, I grew much closer to my children than I imagined was possible.

A day at the zoo with Johnny and Alexis

Though Joe was still very present as their father twice a month and on holidays, I continued to struggle on and off with low self-worth and an intense desire for a godly partner to raise my children with. Little did I know God would answer my prayer several years later by bringing a kind, loving, Christian man named Gus into our lives who would work hard to win my children's hearts and be the role model he felt they needed.

After we married, the years flew by. Before I knew it, Johnny and Alexis were teenagers. As their high school graduations neared, I found my heart filling with tremendous fear about them leaving for college and life beyond our home. I was proud of them and their many accomplishments, but was very unsure about my own future. What would I do when they were no longer the center of my life? Who was I without them?

As God worked in me, I came to realize that when I first married at eighteen, my focus was on the beauty and joy of the wedding ceremony and reception. I had failed to see how very different Joe and I were, despite the love we felt for one another.

With Gus, I understood that marriage takes two people, fully committed, choosing every day to love and respect each other. Rarely does 50/50 describe a successful marriage. The percentages ebb and flow based on the responsibilities, health, and well-being of each partner. A covenant, Christ-centered marriage looks more like 100/100, with both spouses seeking first to serve the other, to support and encourage each other's hopes and dreams.

Yet there is also a parent/child relationship that I would describe as a 100/50, or even 100/20 ratio, with parents fulfilling the 100 percent side. My ratio with Johnny and Alexis probably resembled 100/20, as my fierce mother-love and protection caused me to delight in serving them every chance I could. How I prayed they would never live too far from home so I could continue to be an active part of their lives.

As I struggled with the approaching reality of my children leaving for college, I had no idea God was preparing me for the reality of Johnny leaving *forever*. Nor could I have realized the renewed friendship Johnny's father, Joe, and I would experience following Johnny's death.

Alexis and I grieved side by side, taking small steps each day toward healing, letting the tears flow whenever they wanted to, and spending time alone or with friends when we thought a little distraction might help. For me, spending time in God's Word crying out for comfort, direction, peace, and strength kept me most grounded.

Then, ten days after Johnny died, I received more heartbreaking news. The caller told me that Joe was dead. He, like Johnny, was in a one-car accident that he did not survive.

All I could do was ask, "What? He's dead? How? Why?"

Gus jumped up and immediately left to go to the scene to help any way he could.

I couldn't believe it was happening again so soon after we buried our son. How was I supposed to tell Alexis that her father was dead, too?

I'll never forget walking into her room feeling like it was a chamber of death. I was the carrier of more tragic news. With no easy way to share our latest loss, I sat on the floor beside her and said, "There's been an accident, and your dad didn't make it."

She began to scream, "Why is this happening? Everyone I love is dying! I just want to go to heaven, too!"

Her announcement shocked and terrified me. My own heart was breaking, too, but here my daughter was screaming that she wanted to go to heaven. What might she try to do? Would she be strong enough to overcome the pain she was feeling so soon after losing her brother?

As in the past, I called Eugene, and he and his wife raced over to comfort us both.

I am grateful to God, to Eugene and his wife, and to so many others who have reached out to me and my daughter to help us through months of grief.

The first question we always seem to ask after a tragedy is "Why?" But after experiencing the depth of loss that we did in a matter of days, I believe God allows us to be in situations that we can't handle in our own strength because He wants us to lean on Him.

He wants us to believe that He is who He says He is. He has the power to strengthen and empower us to survive impossible pain. And, in His love, He promises to bring good from every hurt, every weakness, every failure, and every lost dream if we love Him and trust Him to do so.

Johnny and I had a very special relationship. We talked openly about our thoughts and feelings, laughed at the silliest things, and loved to play jokes on one another. My relationship with Alexis is no different. It seems as though the trials of life give us opportunities to either turn our backs on God or dig further into His Word to connect with Him and others on a deeper level.

Children are one of God's greatest blessings. Our relationships with them can withstand the tragedies of life, and even grow stronger, if we cling to God Who promises to never leave us or forsake us.

Through my divorce from my children's father, my son's untimely death, and the death of their dad soon after, Alexis and I have leaned on God and on each other. We have grown decidedly stronger individually and as mother and daughter.

We now know that if we focus on our pain, we lose sight of God. And we decided to be authentic with others about our pain—to let His love and light shine through the cracks of our broken hearts so that others will, perhaps, trust that God has a plan for them beyond their brokenness and pain, too.

Four

Discover Your Path to Passion and Purpose

God Renews, Redeems, and Restores

"For I know the plans I have for you,
says the LORD.
They are plans for good and not for disaster,
to give you a future and a hope."
~ *Jeremiah 29:11*

Helping others has always been a passion of mine. I still remember, as a young girl, having a heart to rock babies born to drug-addicted mothers at hospitals. I assumed they had no one else to hold them and sing to them, and I knew from personal experience how desperately we all need to be loved.

Before I got the chance to rock those babies, however, I married and started a family of my own. We both worked full time to pay our bills and basically got lost in the everyday stress and busyness of life. Fortunately, I had two babies at home to rock, so my desire to help others transformed into a passion to serve my family.

As Johnny and Alexis matured, I knew my job of helping my children was coming to an end, but I had no idea what the future would look like. As young as he was, Johnny knew his purpose and spent countless hours working toward it.

Johnny with his favorite necklace

Without hesitation, he tutored other kids and helped them become better people and perform better in school. His passion and independence affected me and caused me to yearn for a purpose of my own. I wanted to feel like I was accomplishing something worthwhile, too.

It wasn't until Johnny died that I began to sense God speaking to my heart and leading me, step-by-step, down an unfamiliar path that I never would have thought to walk. To be honest, even if I had thought of it, I don't think I would have had the courage to pursue it without the support of the wonderful people God has raised up to mentor, encourage and inspire me.

It all began when Johnny passed away and we started the *LiveLikeJohnny* organization. Its purpose is to continue the legacy that Johnny lived—a legacy of caring for kids who are often left out, ignored, or neglected. His personal mission was to do everything in his power to use his talents, skills, and abilities to change the lives of others in a positive and inspirational way. He longed for people to know they mattered.

Because of Johnny's leadership and personal involvement with our local and area Future Farmers of America (FFA), our initial goal at *LiveLikeJohnny* was to gift FFA jackets to kids in the organization whose families could not afford to purchase one, as Johnny did.

The FFA is a dynamic youth organization that makes a positive difference in the lives of students by developing their potential for premier leadership, personal growth, and career success through agricultural education.

The FFA jacket carries significant value and respect. For some kids, wearing the jacket is only a dream because of financial limitations beyond their control. This is one of our organization's top goals—to make sure that every student who desires to wear the FFA jacket can, by being nominated by those who are aware of their need for assistance.

Johnny and fellow officers in official FFA dress

Johnny was also very passionate about setting and achieving goals within the FFA, and was well known for his accomplishments and awards in that organization. One of his greatest goals was to be elected National FFA President, which he was on his way to becoming prior to his accident.

Through *LiveLikeJohnny*, we also began a scholarship fund to help kids who align with Johnny's personal mission to support those who are neglected, so they have an opportunity to discover and utilize their potential. To that end, we are in the process of developing a mentor program to provide students with support and encouragement as they set goals and work diligently to accomplish them.

We are very proud of what God started through *Live-LikeJohnny*, and we're excited to see where the organization goes from here. But God has even more for us to do, and He is using Johnny's legacy to begin another chapter in my life.

Seven months after Johnny passed away, I was asked to speak at the Texas FFA State Convention in Corpus Christi. It is the largest youth-led convention in the nation, hosting more than 12,000 FFA members and guests … definitely new territory for me since the attendance is roughly three times that of the total population of Jacksboro.

Before I arrived at the convention my mentor and friend, Aaron, asked if I would mind sharing a room with Dawn, another friend of his who was also scheduled to speak. I had met her once before and thought it might be fun to get to know her better, so I said it would be fine.

Me speaking at the *LiveLikeJohnny* gala

That night in our room, we talked and cried and laughed for hours. We connected immediately as though we had known each other all of our lives. At one point, I confessed to her that I was simply walking by faith each day because I felt so completely lost without Johnny.

Then I told her about an idea I had, and she gave me a funny look like she thought I was crazy. It got awkward for a moment as she just stared at me.

Then she opened her mouth and said, "Girl, have you told anyone about this?"

I shook my head and said, "No. Not yet."

"Well, you better trademark that and run with it. It's a great idea. Don't tell anyone about it yet."

"What? You think so?" I replied, stunned.

Later, as we snuggled into our beds, yawning between words, she made me promise again that I would not tell a soul.

I said, "Okay," and fell sound asleep.

The next day we were sitting at lunch with Aaron when Dawn mentioned my idea.

Aaron said, "What are you talking about?"

Dawn wrinkled her nose and raised her hands, palms up.

"He doesn't know," I said. "You told me not to tell anyone, remember?"

"What? It's Aaron!" she said loudly.

I shrugged and shared my idea with him as I had with Dawn the previous night. When I finished, he gave me the same "you must be crazy" look that she had.

What I told them both was this: I had heard of several Christian women who wrote Scripture in their shoes, or had stickers with Scripture on them that they tucked inside their shoes, to help them remember that God is always with them and His Word is powerful and true.

That's how the idea was birthed. I felt called to create inspirational insoles to remind people of God's promises and empower them to believe we truly can do all things in Christ.

My faith in Jesus Christ is what sustained me and gave me the courage and strength to go on after tragedies like my son's death. I want to be constantly reminded of the promises of God. What better way to do that than to literally stand on them?

After I rambled on and on, I paused and took a deep breath, releasing the air with a great sigh.

"Do you think it's a bad idea?" I asked, praying he would say no.

He shook his head. "Not at all. I wish I had thought of it."

I smiled as the three of us began to brainstorm the possibilities. We even thought of a name—*Standing on His Promises,* which later became *Heart InSouls*: Scripture-inspired insoles for all kinds of shoes, with a plan to offer custom insoles for weddings and other special occasions that would include a personal message or favorite Bible verse and the date of the occasion.

I felt so inspired. I couldn't wait to get home and get to work. I also wanted to share the idea with Gus, assuming he would be just as excited as I was. The idea fit so beautifully with the organization we started to honor Johnny's legacy, that we decided a percentage of profits would be contributed to *LiveLikeJohnny* to help fund an increasing number of scholarships and gift more FFA jackets to kids in need.

On the way home I could think of nothing else. I was inspired by God with an idea, and I was encouraged by two friends who thought it was pretty good. We had brainstormed an initial plan, and I believed it would be wonderfully received.

But the longer I thought about our conversations, the responsibilities, and potential for disaster, the more fearful I became. Who was I to think I could start and run a business? What if my idea ended up being a failure like other ideas and decisions in my past? Would *Heart InSouls* become a viable business, or would I end up hiding from embarrassment when it didn't work out?

Aaron and Dawn helped me understand the logistics and legalities as best they could, but I knew I'd also need a lot of time, patience, prayer… and money. I suddenly felt like I was in over my head, and had no idea where to turn.

When I got home, I told Gus about it, but didn't receive the support I had hoped for. He is a practical man, and my idea sounded crazy to him. I had only told three people about my idea. I was afraid the first two would think I was crazy, but they loved it. I hoped my husband would support me without question, but he ended up being the one who couldn't grasp the potential of my idea. He's the person who knows me best, who has promised to love me, had a child with me, and shares every day with me—and *he's* the one who ended up thinking the idea was crazy.

It made me think of the verse in the Bible when Jesus says that a prophet is not honored in his own hometown (John 4:44). I'm no prophet, but when Jesus walked the earth, people knew He was a carpenter, the son of Joseph and Mary, two very ordinary people; so they had a difficult time recognizing Him as the Son of God, or even believing it could be true.

A year has passed since that day, and *Heart InSouls* is in business. I have felt overwhelmed at times, but I constantly pray for God to be with me. In the midst of everything, I am reminded that it's not my business. It's God's, and He has a wonderful plan for it, which takes a lot of pressure off me.

To my surprise, God has placed the right people in the right place at the right time to bring the idea He gave me to completion. Matthew 7:7 says, "Ask, and it will be given to you; seek, and you will find; knock, and it will be opened to you." Boy, have I asked and knocked a lot in the past couple of years!

I have learned time and again how much more effective and rewarding it is to do things God's way. Each time I tried to move my new business forward by myself without prayer, I hit a bump in the road. But when I stopped to pray and meditate on Scripture, the phone would ring or

I would talk to someone who just happened to know the answer to my questions or know someone who did.

God has truly blessed me on this journey by introducing me to amazing people who have donated time, money, and talent to help *Heart InSouls* get off the ground. In spite of the incredible darkness and pain I have endured the past sixteen months, I have had the opportunity to sit in His Word and allow it to comfort and heal my hurting heart. Because of extensive time with God, I have also been sensitized in my spirit to recognize more clearly when He is leading me. His love and my faith in His power to heal has helped me turn my pain into new passion.

I can't claim that I've had full support from some people whom I dearly love, but I believe so strongly in the vision God has given me with *Heart InSouls* that I can't turn my back on it. My husband and I have not been in agreement since I first had the idea, and I respect his opinion and his desire for me to return to full-time employment. Our family needs me to contribute to our finances.

It is true that a steady routine Monday through Friday has been known to help people restore their emotional foundation after experiencing a loss or living with depression. In addition, I initially struggled with the thought that I was not honoring my husband. But because I was convinced that I was honoring God, I moved forward. I had to give the business a chance.

Heart in the clouds—God's gift to me when I doubted His plan for *Heart InSouls*

So here we are, launching what began as a thought that was nurtured by godly men and women into a full-grown business that I am very proud to be part of.

The vision for *Heart InSouls* is to empower, connect, and support people across the globe with a comforting reminder of God's promises. How can we go wrong by doing what is right in the eyes of God?

My passion is not to develop and run another profit-driven machine and add to our country's massive amount of consumer footwear. My passion is to honor God by creating comfortable insoles that bring hope and peace to every person who wears them by reminding them through the Scripture in their shoes that God loves them and has a wonderful plan for their lives.

Proverbs 3:6 says, "In all your ways acknowledge Him, and He will direct your paths." The insoles we offer have had that specific verse prayed over them—that each person who wears them will sense the direction and path God is leading them to follow.

Because a percentage of the profit from *Heart InSouls* will be donated to the *LiveLikeJohnny* organization, I get to follow my new God-given passion and help support my son's legacy organization as well.

Losing Johnny has led me to look at life with gratitude and appreciation. I value each day more than I ever have. I missed so much of Johnny's and Alexis's young lives because I was a single mom who had to work and couldn't be with them. I don't want that to be the case anymore. I want to be able to work as much as possible, but also be available for my children when they need me. In addition to Johnny and Alexis, Gus and I have a three-year-old son named Grant, and I want to be present as he learns new skills and tries new things as he grows.

Family is my top priority, after my relationship with Jesus. My parents aren't getting any younger either, and I want to take care of them as they have taken care of me. Ultimately, I want to be who God created me to be!

So many of us twist ourselves into knots, desperately trying to be someone we were never intended to be. We try to match the skills and accomplishments of women who are gourmet chefs, company presidents, Bible-study leaders, and former beauty-pageant contestants, thinking we will, somehow, feel more worthy of love and belonging. I know how exhausting it is to live like that, because I tried.

Most of my life I attempted to meet and exceed the expectations of others. Sadly, many of us allow the world to define what it means to be a woman, to be a success, and to live a valuable life. But we have been deceived. Instead of living a life of authenticity, sincerity, and purpose, we've been consumed with striving to live up to the world's definition of perfection and success.

Do you know any perfect women who are gorgeous, fit, wealthy, drive a luxury car, live in a spotless house in the best neighborhood in town, own and run their own profitable business, and raise perfect well-mannered children who adore them? I'm exhausted just writing that description, much less thinking about trying to become that woman. Yet haven't we all been deluded at some point, thinking we just might pull it off?

It took me close to forty years to figure out that the world's definition of just about anything is way off. There is no life in trying to fit in or compete or pretend to be what we know deep inside we are not.

Real joy is only found in being honest with ourselves and others and pursuing only what we sense God leading us to. He's the only one who knows how the gifts and talents He planted in us will best serve the world and lead us to the kind of success He knows will bring us ultimate joy.

When was the last time you asked God what He's up to in your life? Who has He created you to be? What do you need to remove from your schedule in order to reclaim the unique parts of yourself that God plans to use in ways that will astonish you if you let Him?

As Pastor Rick Warren wrote, "God formed every creature on this planet with a special area of expertise. Some animals run, some hop, some swim, some burrow, and some fly. Each has a particular role to play, based on the way they were shaped by God. The same is true with humans. Each of us is uniquely designed, or 'shaped,' to do certain things. . . . This means nothing that happens in your life is insignificant. God uses all of it to mold you for your ministry to others and shape you for your service to Him."

Isn't it awesome to know that God created you with specific abilities, interests, talents, gifts, personality, and life experiences to train you and lead you to embrace *His* definition of success which, by the way, is guaranteed to fill you with the greatest joy and purpose possible because He knows you best?

Five

Focus on Your True Foundation

In Christ, You Have the Power to Succeed

"Yes, I am the vine; you are the branches.
Those who remain in me, and I in them,
will produce much fruit."
~ *John 15:5*

My parents gifted me with a firm foundation of faith, though I wasn't always a big fan of it. No matter how late we had been out the night before, we were required to get up for church on Sunday morning. We used to joke that we'd have to be on our deathbed to avoid Sunday service.

Though unconventional, my mom would attempt to wake us by playing the piano at an ear-splitting level. If that didn't work, she would come into our rooms and try to tease us out of our sleep. If we still didn't respond, she would start to scream until we crawled out from under the sheets.

My parents continue to be very religious to this day, and I am so grateful for the foundation they laid and the example they set for us as a family. It wasn't until I had to face the loss of my son that I recognized how critical that foundation was to my ability to survive.

Though I claimed Jesus as my Lord and Savior and I prayed to God, I realized after Johnny's accident that I had never really allowed God to take control of my life. I was living for myself and for what I thought I wanted out of life. In the midst of my intense grief, however, I sincerely surrendered to God and invited the Holy Spirit to guide me.

Today I can't imagine a life that is void of God's unconditional love and support. When everything seemed to be falling apart after the accident, God stayed very close and kept me from being consumed by my brokenness.

The Bible says in Psalm 30:5, "Weeping may last through the night, but joy comes with the morning." Though it took much longer than one night to restore even a hint of joy to my heart, I knew I could believe God's promise and trust that one day my joy would return. My heart still aches, and probably always will, but God *is* bringing joy from my anguish one day at a time.

No matter what you believe you have lost, God is there for you, too. No matter how broken you feel, you can always find something to be thankful for and people whose support you can be grateful to have.

If you have children, it's usually a good place to start. After Johnny passed, I fell into a very dark place for six months and struggled each day to get out.

I felt emotionally fragile and was constantly fatigued. I couldn't imagine facing another problem or demand on my time. Because I was unable to think straight, I felt like I couldn't do anything right. My mind was simply incapable of focusing on anything but my loss.

Where Johnny was laid to rest

Then God opened my eyes and helped me recognize that I still have a daughter and a young son to raise. They need me, and I need them. They are a significant blessing and reason to heal and grow strong.

I am also married, and though we don't always see eye to eye—as I'm sure most married people don't—we are partners in life, and his presence and support allow me to spend precious time with God and pursue the path God is calling me to walk.

Do you have a career? A passion for something creative, beautiful, and meaningful to you? If so, it is one of God's greatest blessings. We don't want to deny our grief, but having a place to go to invest our time and talent is a very positive thing. Don't try to rush the grief process, but do trust that God knows everything, including your pain, and He has a plan to bring something beautiful from it.

I imagine many of you are like I was, struggling with self-esteem and self-image issues, not understanding how to love yourself the way you are and accept that you are beautiful and worthy in the eyes of God. You may even feel like you've done too many things wrong and made too many bad decisions for God to forgive you and love you. But thankfully, that way of thinking is simply not true. If He forgave me, and I am confident He did, then He will forgive you, too.

I still can't believe how God led me to the idea for *Heart InSouls* and continues to lead me to others who want to help build its foundation and sustain its future. Because of what God is doing for me through my grief, I want to encourage you and fill you with hope to trust that something wonderful is waiting for you, too, on the other side of your grief. And I will be here to cheer you on when God has made it clear to you exactly what that purpose is.

God chose you a long time ago, before He sent Jesus, His Son, to earth to die as payment for all of our sins. The Bible says all you need to do is believe in your heart that Jesus is the Son of God and say with your mouth, "Jesus is Lord," and you will be saved.

It's that simple. Believe, repent, receive God's forgiveness, and you become part of His family destined to live forever in heaven with Him. Knowing I will be reunited with Johnny in heaven one day fills me with tremendous peace and joy.

In the meantime, I talk to my mom every day. She knows me so well she can tell when something is wrong without me saying a word. I am so grateful for her love and support. I'm also blessed with several friends who I can be completely honest with and trust to hold my deepest feelings and fears in strictest confidence.

Who are the people in your life worthy of that kind of trust? Who supports and listens to you, encouraging you to be authentic with your thoughts and feelings, loving you no matter what you say or do?

The freedom to be wholly myself with my family and friends is priceless, yet in the midst of my pain it was difficult for me to share some of my darkest thoughts out of fear they would not be able to understand. Those were the times I was most grateful for my foundation of faith in God.

Ultimately, the only one we can be brutally honest with is God. He is ever-aware of our thoughts and feelings, and He chooses to love us unconditionally anyway. We have no reason *not* to be honest with Him, though He's not always easy to find. It actually makes me crazy sometimes that I can't grasp His hand or see His face to connect in the way I am used to connecting with people on earth.

Yet I believe with all of my heart that He is here and He is perfectly capable of having a deep and fulfilling relationship with us through His Holy Spirit. It is my profound personal relationship with God that spoke to my heart after Johnny and his biological father passed within ten days of each other. Losing them both was incredibly difficult, but I was comforted by the thought that Johnny's dad would be with Johnny in heaven, along with a child we lost early in our marriage.

The Bible says that God knows us before we are conceived. He knits us together in our mothers' wombs, and all of our days are numbered in His Book of Life before we take our first breath. Those truths are included in Psalm 139, one of the most beautiful and hopeful of all of the psalms.

As long as we have God and His Word, we have the most powerful support and comfort available on earth. With the help of the Holy Spirit, our eyes are opened wider when we experience loss, and our hearts become more capable of grasping the gift of gratitude.

Since Johnny passed, I see things I never noticed before, and I appreciate the beauty and creativity of creation like I never did. The wind astounds me. Where does it begin and end? Bird songs lift my spirit. How many different songs do they sing? Sunrises and sunsets: were they always so stunning with their vibrant bands of color?

I had no idea what I was missing in the busyness of life, but I am now deeply aware of everyday simple gifts from God, for which I am grateful.

Sunrise with a cross in the sky on the one-year anniversary of Johnny's burial

What about you? What blessings can you thank God for despite your pain and loss? Do you believe God loves you and has gifted you with specific talents and gifts, and that He has a wonderful plan for your life?

Remember, as Psalm 30:5 so compassionately reminds us, "Weeping may last through the night, but joy comes with the morning."

God knows what you are going through. He knows why you are hurting. He knows what or who caused the pain. God understands even your deepest inexpressible feelings. Whatever you are going through, let me assure you that God is working something out for your good.

At the right time, He will restore everything you have lost. He will mend your broken heart. He will renew your fainting spirit. He will wipe away your tears. He will put joy in your heart and a smile on your face.

Proclaim "I trust in God, so why should I be afraid? What can mere mortals do to me?" (Psalm 56:11).

Six

Find Happiness in Your Healing

Choose Joy

"…you have sorrow now,
but I will see you again,
and your hearts will rejoice,
and no one will take your joy from you."
~ John 16:22

"Everything happens for a reason."

"It will get better with time."

"You need to move on."

I heard each one of those comments, and more, as people tried to motivate me to will myself out of my grief. I knew they meant well. They were worried about me. But more than that, I think they were uncomfortable around me. They didn't know what to say, so they thought if they could get me to move on, they would be able to return to life with me as they knew it before Johnny's accident.

What they didn't realize, however, was that the more they pushed me to heal, the more the pain intensified inside me. Because of their comments, I began to feel like there was something wrong with me—like perhaps I was being unreasonable with my own expectation of grieving by not moving through the "stages" fast enough. So I began to hide my real feelings and pretend like I was the perfectly normal person they wanted me to be.

The fact is, maybe grieving my son's death alone would have caused me to move through the various stages of grief a bit quicker than I was able to, but Johnny's death wasn't the only loss I was grieving.

With Johnny's and my daughter's biological father's tragic death just ten days after Johnny's accident, I wasn't given the opportunity and freedom to grieve as another parent might grieve. My sixteen-year-old daughter needed my comfort and support. She needed me to be strong while she felt weak.

A month later, Alexis appeared to be dealing with her grief as best she could. I thought I might get to sink back into my own grief, but then we were told her boyfriend passed away from an accidental death. There's a saying about bad things coming in threes, but why to the same family? Why *our* family?

Pain was being piled on top of pain. Grief on top of grief. And the fear of what might happen next began to fill my thoughts. I was on grief overload, unable to process much beyond the fact that I felt completely lost.

My emotions alternated between fear, rage, sadness, what-ifs, and loneliness. I felt like I was sleepwalking through life, physically present but emotionally distant. I was afraid I was losing my mind as I struggled to remember the simplest things.

Here's a brief description of the stages of grief as I understand them, though I bounced around at different times, feeling depression and despair one day, then shock or intense concern the next. Grieving is very personal, but as a general rule these are the stages we all go through after experiencing loss.

Shock and Denial – Shock is the initial reaction to loss. Shock is the person's emotional protection from being too suddenly overwhelmed by the loss. The person may not yet be willing or able to believe what their mind knows to be true. This stage normally lasts two or three months.

Intense Concern – Intense concern often manifests by rendering a person unable to think of anything else. Even during daily tasks, thoughts of the loss keep coming to mind. Conversations with someone at this stage always turn to the loss, as well. This period may last from six months to a year.

Despair and Depression – Despair and depression is the most painful and protracted stage for someone who is grieving. It is the stage where the person gradually comes to terms with the reality of the loss. The process typically involves a wide range of feelings, thoughts, and behaviors. Many behaviors may be irrational. Depression can include feelings of anger, guilt, sadness, and anxiety.

Recovery – The goal of grieving is not the elimination of all the pain or the memories of the loss. In this stage, the person shows a new interest in daily activities and begins to function more normally day by day. At the end of the grieving process, the hope is that the person reorganizes their life so the loss is an important part of their life rather than the center of it.

Every step of the grief process is natural and healthy. It's only when a person gets stuck in one step, or stage, for a long period of time that the grieving can become unhealthy, destructive, and even dangerous.

No specific timeline for grief works for everyone. The only thing I know for sure is that it takes time, and when we don't have enough time to grieve one significant loss before another loss occurs, we end up emotionally overwhelmed and unable to give any of the losses the attention they deserve.

The hardest part for me was being surrounded by people who thought they knew how I needed to grieve. The pain my daughter was suffering after losing her brother, her father, and her boyfriend in a forty-five-day period of time seemed to be far greater than mine.

I have a strong faith. I knew I would be okay, because God's Word promises that He is close to the brokenhearted and saves those who are crushed in spirit (Psalm 34:18). He will never leave nor forsake us (Deuteronomy 31:6). That doesn't mean it wasn't difficult. It was life changing. But my daughter's young heart was forever etched with a canyon of loss at a tender age, and that broke my heart even more.

Two weeks after we attended our third funeral, Alexis and I had to begin the process of settling her father's estate. I had no idea how to help a sixteen-year-old navigate not only the material aspect of settling his estate, but the emotional aspect as well. At night I would hear her crying in her room, alone. I yearned to go to her and hold her, but I didn't know how to comfort her when I was so broken myself.

At that point, I started to avoid the phone, preferring to send even calls from my friends to voicemail. Casual conversations began to annoy and frustrate me. They seemed so trivial at the time. Now I realize I hurt many of my friends because I pushed them away, but I didn't intend to.

It was all part of my grieving process. I needed to be alone, and didn't know how to communicate that to anyone else.

Alexis grieved differently. She needed time to cry and be alone, but she also possesses an inner strength that can shine through any tragedy or difficult circumstance. She has always radiated an energy and light that is impossible to ignore. I admire her and the way she handled her grief with such grace.

I, on the other hand, am not sure how much grace was involved in my healing. Trying to grieve while I was home with a three-year-old was not exactly easy. I wanted so much to be alone, but with a beautiful little boy to care for, I couldn't shut everything and everyone out of my life.

Despite sending phone calls to voicemail, I had no choice but to be involved in my husband's and children's lives, to take care of them and fulfill as many of my responsibilities at home as I could. Perhaps that's why I feel like my path from shock to recovery took longer than it might normally have taken if I had had time alone to process each loss individually.

Grieving multiple losses at the same time taught me the simple truth that we grieve each loss in a unique way based on how long we knew them, how close we were, and how meaningful our relationship was. Johnny's death was, of course, the most difficult, but his father's death was hard, too. He was the father of my two oldest children, and we were married for eight years. Because of that, he was still part of our lives.

Another truth I learned is that no matter how strong your faith is, it doesn't mean you won't question it at some point in the grieving process. Satan knows when we are most vulnerable, and he takes advantage of that by trying to manipulate our thoughts and feelings to the point that they become very real to us.

We can begin to question if, perhaps, we are experiencing grief because we did something so bad that God decided to punish us by taking someone we love from us. I, for one, struggled with that as I walked through despair and depression following Johnny's death.

Then, as only God can do, He spoke to my heart in the most loving way and began to transform my thoughts. He led me to His Word in which David, Paul, and so many others state that God is loving and kind and faithful and merciful and so good that He takes the most tragic situations and turns them into something magnificent.

I know it's difficult to imagine feeling joyful again when you're in the midst of your grief. In my case, experiencing so much loss and grief at the same time turned me inside out. It was as though a bomb exploded in my heart and mind and left nothing but chaos and disaster. Nothing feels the same anymore. You have no idea how to begin to put things back together. You are, frankly, not even sure you can.

It feels a lot like my daughter's room, with clothes, papers, shoes, hangers, blankets, and pillows tossed all over every inch of what would be a restful place if it were clean. I'm not sure anymore what it looked like before the hurricane hit, but I can dream. Walking past her room can feel overwhelming. I want to clean it for her, but I don't know where to begin.

Loss can feel exactly like that. It's overwhelming and exhausting, and people who love you wish they could swoop in and sweep every hint of loneliness, sadness, and despair far away. But they can't.

I wouldn't know how to help or where to put things in my daughter's room, and others can't clean up the mess inside of us when we're hurting. Only the love of Jesus can do that. He is the only one who can take us by the hand and lead us to what the Bible calls the peace that passes all understanding (Philippians 4:4–7).

Some of the most difficult encounters for me to endure after my loss were the countless questions people would ask when they saw me. "How are you? Are you okay?" and others that I had no easy answers for. Sometimes I felt like screaming, "How in the world could I possibly be okay?" but I held my tongue, and I am so glad I did.

I realize now that people were uncomfortable. They didn't know what to say. They wanted to be supportive and help if they could. I'm sure I asked the same questions of grieving people in the past before I suffered my own intense loss.

Today I am extremely thankful for the people who cared enough to ask how I was and how my family was doing. It was my grief that kept me from appreciating their concern at the time.

Whatever you do, don't stuff your grief and think for a minute that you can live or function … or heal. If you try to deny what you feel, you will remain emotionally broken and will likely live a life filled with fear. Fear of losing someone else. Fear of allowing yourself to love deeply again. Fear of trying anything new because you may fail and cast yourself further down into a pit of despair.

Instead of stuffing your feelings, talk with others who understand—most importantly, God. But also consider a counselor or a support group. You may even have friends or family members who are gifted listeners who have a desire to walk the path to recovery with you.

And don't forget to breathe. I was amazed how I would literally hold my breath or breathe so shallowly that my body was negatively impacted without me realizing. My shoulders were tense, my stomach was tied in continual knots, and my chest felt like it could explode at any moment from the pain I was holding inside.

It's a simple but critical practice. Before you read further, take a deep breath and hold it for three seconds, then release the air. You may want to do it several times, in fact. Feel the tension release? It's amazing how something so simple can help reduce the stress, anxiety, and pain we experience in the midst of grief, and in many other situations.

Last, I don't think I would have been able to survive so many losses without the people in my life who made me laugh without even trying. That may sound a bit callous, but studies have proven that humor is a tremendous tool to help people cope with illness and loss.

In my case, humor got me through some of my toughest days. Grief can suck all of the joy out of life and make everything around you feel dark. It may be a long time before you find something to laugh about, but I promise that day will come, and it will be good for you. Don't feel guilty for smiling or laughing again. It's a positive part of the healing process.

You will experience the greatest joy of recovery when you realize you made it past the place where memories of the one you lost make you feel nothing but sad. When you can laugh while sharing crazy, loving, warm, fun, generous, weird, and stubborn stories about your loved one, you have gotten to a very good place.

My son, Johnny, epitomized every one of those descriptions, and more. When I think of him and the joy he brought us, I smile and thank God for the time he was with us on earth.

Our first family photo after Johnny passed

I think we've all heard the phrase, "Happiness is a choice." I'm not sure I agreed with that until after Johnny died. Until then, I was convinced that happiness was a by-product of an easy life that included a healthy family, loving relationships, and enough money to buy most anything I wanted.

Now I see that if life is that easy, happiness doesn't require a choice. It's when life is difficult that we need to choose happiness, or joy, as the Bible refers to it.

You see, when I was pregnant with Johnny, his dad and I witnessed a horrific accident on the way to Decatur. A car in front of us flew into the air, and when it landed, caught the driver in its twisted metal and broke her in half. Her passenger was ejected from the car and landed beside our truck.

I ran over to the passenger to see if I could comfort her. She looked directly into my eyes before she died. I grabbed my stomach and immediately thought about the family she left behind. How, I wondered, would they survive without her? How could they ever be happy again knowing their daughter was gone?

I still have dreams of that girl, and I pray for John, the man who found my son and stayed with him. I am so grateful Johnny was not physically alone when he passed. Tragedies like that can change us. I know they changed me.

Happiness no longer requires ease or perfection, popularity or wealth, or anything else I once thought necessary. Now I realize that we all get to choose how we react to the circumstances of our lives. After Johnny died, I chose to lean on God and trust that His Word is true when it promises "joy in the morning…" *after* the weeping.

Life is too precious to waste choosing anything but joy. I pray you will decide today to make the most of the beautiful messed-up life you may have. Let go of everything that holds you back so you can hold on to what matters most. Happiness *is* a choice

"Super Grant" with me and Alexis at Halloween

Grief is agonizing. It's like having heart surgery with no anesthesia and then being told two days later that you need to return to work and get your life together.

The truth is, my life will never be the same. I have a constant companion called grief, and the emotions erupt when I least expect it. People say there will be days like that, but I know that *every* day will be one of those days for me.

Because my son was part of my soul, a tear hides behind every smile. And I'm okay with that, because God promises to reunite us in heaven one day, and we will live forever in a place where there are no more tears or sickness or death.

That's what gives me confidence to choose joy! I pray you will choose it too.

Christmas—holding Johnny close in our hearts

Seven

Transform Obstacles into Opportunites

You Can Win the Battle Within

"This is my command—be strong and courageous!
Do not be afraid or discouraged.
For the LORD your God is with you
wherever you go."
~ *Joshua 1:9*

In His Word, God promises to never leave or forsake us as we pursue the dreams He has placed in our hearts. But someone else is also acutely aware of our hopes and dreams, and he is trying to do everything he can to destroy our dreams and pull us away from Christ.

The battle is real. It is the reason so many believers live in defeat and lack the joy God intends for us to possess and share with the world.

Now that you know most of my story, you can appreciate and maybe even connect with much of the loss and failure I experienced. Because of my past, Satan has always known exactly how to attack me, where my soft spots are, and the areas where I am most likely to fall into despair. And he knows yours too.

As Joyce Meyer says in *Win the Battle with Power Thoughts*, "You're not crazy if you talk to yourself. In fact, your thoughts are 'talking' to you all the time. And the way you talk to yourself is one of the most important things in your life. You can never get beyond what you think—especially what you think of yourself."

It took me most of my life to realize that truth. I still struggle at times in my mind today and am amazed at the impact my thoughts have had on my success or failure.

Satan began to attack my young heart and mind by making me feel unworthy at home and at school. Then he continued his well-placed attacks throughout my life, causing me to make numerous decisions that ended in regret. He also used unsuspecting people to plant doubt and fear inside me to keep me from pursuing my passions, which led me to feel like a failure.

How has he attacked you? Has he consistently used the same method, person, or group of people to make you feel unworthy of success? Are you terrified to be who you really are and say what you truly feel because you fear rejection? Does a diminished sense of self-worth keep you from taking risks for fear you will fail and go into hiding from embarrassment or humiliation?

I have often heard if we want to live a life of happiness, we have to change the way we think. I used to believe it was next to impossible for anyone to do that, but now I realize we can control our thoughts if we focus on God and all the good things He represents.

The first time I recognized I had some power over my thoughts is when I surrendered control of my life to Christ. The moment I believed in God's love for me and trusted that He had an amazing plan for my life, my attitude and thought life began to shift in a more positive direction.

As I read in the Bible about His promise to make us new creations and give us new life when we surrender our hopes and dreams to Him, my attitudes and thoughts shifted even more. I wish I could say it happened in an instant. I've read that some people have experienced forgiveness and healing and never looked back. They immediately began to walk in freedom and joy, proclaiming the goodness of God.

But my freedom in Christ didn't come quite that fast. I imagine your story is similar to mine. When I first surrendered my life to Christ, I experienced an initial high of receiving God's unconditional love and forgiveness. Then heartaches and failures stepped in, along with Satan and his warfare, and it became easy to succumb to doubt and fear.

Loss is an interesting phenomenon, though. Unlike freedom and forgiveness from sin, pain and grief can resurface when you least expect it, bringing fresh doubt and fear with it. I encourage you not to let it derail you. Grief is love, or rather the experience of lost love. It's normal to feel it from time to time as long as you don't dwell on it.

Think of it like a chart that shows a line moving up ten squares, down five, then up again by eight—an ever-increasing move upward with down days in between. Whatever our path, God already knew what it would look like before we surrendered to Him, so we can rest in that and just keep moving forward with fewer down days as we walk with God.

Sadly, Satan can use our grief to rob us of every dream we've had for our lives. He tries to make us believe there's no reason to hope after our loved one is gone. But he's a liar. You have every reason to draw even closer to God and believe that God will bring beauty from the pain you are enduring.

As the Bible states, every day we *must* "put on all of God's armor so that [we] will be able to stand firm against all strategies of the devil. For we are not fighting against flesh-and-blood enemies, but against evil rulers and authorities of the unseen world, against mighty powers in this dark world, and against evil spirits in the heavenly places" (Ephesians 6:10–12).

Whether we acknowledge it or not, we live in a spiritual war zone, and the primary battle takes place in our hearts and minds. The Bible teaches that every Christian is under spiritual attack. Make no mistake, Satan has his sights fixed squarely on you.

At times, you may feel like you are under constant attack and are failing at winning the battle. I feel this way more often than I would like to admit. Joyce Meyer encourages us by saying, "The great thing about an attitude is that it's yours and you can change it." That's why we need to go to God in daily prayer. We have the power to change our thoughts, but not through our own will.

Meyer also says, "The mind is one of the hardest areas to get under control and keep under control. Part of why it's hard is because Satan will attack you with lies and deceptions. You need to guard yourself against that. . . . You have to believe God's Word is for you. Then you need to hear yourself say what you believe."

And she literally means to hear yourself say what you believe out loud. Here are a few power Scripture phrases to get you started:

"God loves me" (1 John 4:16).

"God has good plans for me" (Jeremiah 29:11).

"God will never leave me" (Deuteronomy 31:6).

"God delights in me and rejoices over me with singing" (Zephaniah 3:17).

"God is my refuge and strength, an ever-present help in trouble" (Psalm 46:1).

"God's thoughts are not like my thoughts. His ways are far beyond anything I could imagine" (Isaiah 55:8).

And so much more. Search the Psalms. Read the Gospels. The Bible is filled with truth and encouragement to pull you out of darkness and despair into abundant life.

Because of my faith, I believe in my heart that God will bring joy and blessing from my many losses. And you can claim His promise, too.

As I clung to God and His Word through my grief, He began to bring people into my life to support and encourage me. Not people who just want to be part of the buzz of a new business or who desire to network for the sake of their own agenda, but people who are truly on my side and who sincerely want to cheer me on to success.

If you want to turn your life into a beautiful story of success, you need to be open to receive whatever—or whomever—God sends your way. I had no preconceived ideas about what might happen with my idea. I wasn't even sure I would share it with anyone. But God opened the door when I met Dawn at the Texas FFA State Convention, and I'm so thankful He filled me with courage to walk through it and share my idea with her.

I pray that He will give you an amazing idea at the right time and surround you with influencers and connectors and people who have talents and skills to complement your own. God unexpectedly provided encouragers for me in the beginning, and He continues to bring talented people into my life today to help build *Heart InSouls* into a profitable business and expand its boundaries beyond anything I could have asked or imagined.

I believe He wants to do the same for you. He is preparing influencers and connectors and people with talents and skills that complement your own. He will nurture your faith and birth your idea in His time, just as He is doing for me.

You have a role to play, though.

Remember earlier in the book when I told you that my friends, Dawn and Aaron, loved my business idea, but my husband was not exactly a fan? Your role is to listen to God.

If at some point you feel certain He is directing you toward the pursuit of your idea, consider sharing it with someone you trust. If you receive encouragement there, ask if they know someone else who might be interested as well. If they are not encouraging, return to God and ask Him for direction, then wait and trust Him to speak to you.

With a few people to fan the flame of your passion, you have all you need to take the next step. As long as you are sure in your own heart and mind that you are following God's will, don't let anyone deter you, even if they are close to you. Your first and most important job is to do the will of God, just as Jesus continually stated He was doing when He was on earth.

Just be certain to cover everything you do and say with prayer, as it's a delicate dance of love and respect between you and the one(s) who do not yet support your dream. Pray that God will open the eyes of their hearts to see clearly what He is doing through you and those who support you.

My only caution is this: be sure to check your motivation. God cares so much more about who we *are* than what we *do*. I wonder if that's one of the reasons He chose to bless me with *Heart InSouls*.

When we lose someone we love, we are reminded of what is most valuable in life. We realize how important meaningful relationships are, and we grasp the brevity and fragility of life with greater clarity. I also think we become more diligent about discerning God's plan for us and discovering the legacy He desires us to leave.

When our hearts are in that soft place, open and surrendered before God, it is the perfect time for Him to heal and bless. God loves to give us the desires of our hearts when we seek Him (Psalm 37:4). And in the midst of grieving, don't most of us spend a lot of time doing just that? Seeking God as we plead for answers to our many questions that begin with *Why?*

I have had a passion to help others my entire life. My heart is so full of love it sometimes feels like a curse. But out of that love, God led me to found *LiveLikeJohnny* with others who want to help continue Johnny's legacy of caring for kids who are often left out, ignored, or neglected.

Then God birthed the idea for *Heart InSouls* in me and trusted me with an opportunity to help others literally stand (and walk and run!) on His promises. As I experience the launch of *Heart InSouls*, I am continually amazed at God's plan and work. He has held my hand every step of the way, and I am so grateful.

Do you have a passion for something specific, or is your passion more general like mine? Do you just love to help others, or are you a gifted artist, teacher, or athlete? Can you analyze or organize more efficiently than most people you know?

Whatever it is, spend an hour or a day talking to God about it. Take a long walk or snuggle into a soft chair and open your heart to whatever God has for you. Write down everything that comes to mind. Keep a running list day-to-day if you prefer, and jot ideas as they float into your conscience.

When a specific idea makes your heart beat fast, do a little research. List all of the positive points you can think of with regard to owning and running that particular business or taking your idea a step further. Begin to plan your path to success.

Then list any perceived obstacles. Does your list include financial obstacles, emotional obstacles, or a lack of knowledge and/or skill? One by one, determine what is in your power to do, whether it is signing up for a class, finding a mentor, or seeking financial advice.

Give everything beyond your control to God. Ask for His direction, and wait to see what He will do. Allow Him to turn your obstacles into opportunities as He leads you where He planned for you to be before you were born.

What I sometimes perceived as a curse—my huge heart of love and intense desire to help others—has become the very thing God has chosen to use to lead me to success. I'm learning how to step outside of my comfort zone on a regular basis and trust that God will either cause me to soar or catch me if I stumble and get me safely to the next place I need to be.

And while making money to pay the bills is a necessity, having available resources to bless others is what brings me the most joy. Money means nothing on its own. It's the value we attach to it and the generosity that flows from it that gives it true meaning, just as knowing who we are and why we're here gives our lives meaning.

If we ask God to help us fight the battle in our minds, along with fighting Satan, the instigator of many of our most damaging thoughts, God promises to transform our thoughts day by day into positive, confident, hopeful messages. When Satan attacks you, smile and say, "Not today," knowing he only attacks those who have a personal relationship with Christ, because Christ is the only one who can save and empower you to live a victorious life.

Believe God's Word. Claim His promises for yourself and your future, and allow them to soak so deeply into your heart and mind that obstacles become nothing more than temporary road blocks on your way to success.

Eight

Embrace Who You Were Created to Be

You Were Created to Shine

"Thank you for making me
so wonderfully complex!
Your workmanship is marvelous…"
~ Psalm 139:14

Walking through intense loss is not for the faint of heart, nor is it the end of your hopes and dreams. Before each of us was born, God saw us. He formed our bodies, hearts, and minds and gave us specific gifts and talents to be used to fulfill His purposes for our lives on earth. We were blessed in unimaginable ways before we took one breath.

All He asks is that we seek Him with all of our hearts so we will be better able to hear His voice and sense with clarity the direction He wants us to go. Where do we begin? How can we know what our natural gifts and talents are? We can start by asking God to show us as we take a personal inventory.

What five things do you enjoy doing the most? In what areas do you excel without strain? What do you think you are naturally good at? What do others comment about? Do they say you are exceptionally thoughtful, kind, or generous? Are you gifted with creativity or blessed with an ability to solve difficult problems?

Next, ask a few people close to you who you believe will be honest with you. What positive traits do they see in you? What talents do they feel come naturally to you? How have they seen God bless others through you?

I spent decades trying to fulfill the expectations of people around me, never taking into account how God specifically gifted me. I just wanted to fit in, not stand out. Unfortunately, that meant I wasn't walking in my gifting, which meant I wasn't living my most meaningful life. I was tied up in knots trying to be who I was never created to be.

Can you relate to that feeling?

Are you successful in areas of your life that others praise you for and are impressed by, but which bring you little to no joy? Have you experienced that in the past? If so, how did you feel? What did you do?

I love reading about surgeons who become missionaries, business owners who sell to follow their dream of teaching or mentoring, and wealthy executives who choose to step down or move into semi-retirement in order to engage in what they are most passionate about.

What do they all have in common? They felt a nagging sense that there was something more. They each recognized, sometimes after years of soul-searching, that what they desired most was to get in touch with who they were created to be and live a life that reflected their authentic nature. No matter how successful they were in the eyes of the world, their hearts remained a bit unsettled until they connected with their God-given passion and gifting.

That's when the magic happens. As St. Irenaeus said, "The glory of God is a man fully alive." Nowhere is this more evident than when you connect with your authentic self. When you do that, you activate God's purpose for you and open the door that leads to the life of passion and purpose God intended you to live all along. While the following quote is variously credited as an Indian proverb, a Tibetan Buddhist proverb, or a Cherokee proverb, it is one that shares a profound thought.

> "When you were born,
> you cried and the world rejoiced.
> Live your life so that when you die,
> the world cries and you rejoice."

Success is important, but more important than that is the impact you make. A lot of people make an impression. Johnny made an impact, and I want to do the same. I want to bless lives, help people develop their talents and gifts, and make the world a better place. I guess you could say I am hoping to live in a way that causes those I have touched to cry at my passing while I rejoice with Jesus in heaven.

There are some powerful objective assessments available online to help you discover your personality, innate abilities (natural talents), and spiritual gifting. I encourage you to check them out. Here are a few I highly recommend:

1. Uniquely You – excellent spiritual gifts assessment with an option to complete a DISC personality profile. Cost varies depending on assessment(s) selected.

2. StrengthsFinder (Clifton Strengths Assessment) – used primarily in the business world, but valuable for anyone seeking to understand their foundational strengths and weaknesses. Wide range of cost beginning at $12.00.

3. The Enneagram – Popular five-minute personality test that helps people understand their inner workings. Used in a variety of spiritual contexts. Free online.

Web sites for assessments are provided in the Resource section at the end of the book.

Have fun discovering your gifts and talents. Share your results with people at work and at church if you feel inclined. Each assessment will move you one step closer to knowing who God created you to be.

I love the subtitle of Rebekah Lyons's book, *You Are Free.* It is *Be Who You Already Are.* Can you imagine a world in which we all took that advice and lived and loved and worked out of our God-given talents and gifting? If we simply chose to be who we already are?

Rebekah exhorts us to be free to grieve, free to confess, free to begin again, and so much more. Isn't that what every human being yearns for whether we realize it or not? It makes sense to me that the likelihood of us living authentically and being who God created us to be would increase exponentially if we took time to learn our strengths, weaknesses, spiritual gifts, and personalities.

Add to that prayer and patience with God's answer, and we've got an excellent chance of not only hearing God's direction, but discerning open doors that we are prepared to walk through because we took the time to discover, in advance, our natural gifts and talents.

I would never have guessed that my God-given talents and gifts would have led me down the winding road that is my life. But as I prepare to launch *Heart InSouls*, I believe every experience inside and outside of work has helped me be ready. I learned from every failure, recovered from every regret, and thanks to God, healed through every loss and have grown stronger and wiser through them.

What did you dream of becoming when you were young? As a teenager, did you fantasize about having a large loving family, inventing a new product, or starting your own business? As the famous saying goes, "What would you do if you knew you would not fail?"

I'm not suggesting you turn your life upside down, though sometimes God intervenes or allows certain circumstances to occur, and that's exactly what happens. In my situation, God called me to surrender my pain and heartache to Him in my father's hospital room, which led me to desire a deeper relationship with God and a more intimate connection through prayer.

Through those years of seeking more of God, my faith dramatically increased to the point that He knew I would struggle greatly after Johnny died, but I would not stop trusting in His goodness and love.

In my brokenness and despair, when my heart was humble and open before God, He chose to plant the seed for *Heart InSouls* in my spirit, knowing in advance I would choose, with encouragement and support of others, to follow His direction. As you know from my story, I had my doubts about starting a new business with little more than an idea, but God confirmed His will over and over and kept me on the right path.

Has God called you out of your comfort zone to lead a small group or start a new business? To speak or write or teach? What have you done with that call? Do you have others to encourage and support you as you step out in faith to do what God is calling you to do?

Remember this—you do not have to worry about being smart enough or beautiful enough or popular enough to accomplish your dreams and your calling in your own strength. God already knows none of us are enough. But Jesus is, and He is worth risking everything for.

When we grieve, Jesus is hope.

When we are afraid, Jesus is brave.

When we are weak, Jesus is strong.

When we are lost, Jesus knows the way.

When we are lonely, Jesus is love.

Because of Jesus, you can breathe deep and rest and wait. There is no hurry with God, no striving in your own strength to become successful in His eyes. He prepares and calls and leads in His time.

I pray you enjoy His presence while you seek His will. And as God makes your path clearer, give Him the glory. Enjoy the ride.

Embrace your gifts and talents. Be who you were created to be! If at first you fail, ask God for clarity and new direction, and when you hear Him speak or sense His leading, try again.

Always remember God's encouragement to Joshua in Joshua 1:9: "This is my command—be strong and courageous! Do not be afraid or discouraged. For the LORD your God is with you wherever you go."

And so it is with you and me. God is with us. Be strong, though you feel weak. Be courageous, though you sometimes doubt God's calling and direction. Be confident, for God promises to be with you wherever you go.

Be like a glow stick. Shine bright because of your brokenness, and praise the God who chooses to use you anyway.

Honoring Johnny's life and legacy

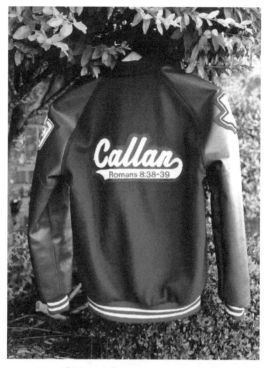

One of Johnny's favorite scriptures that was
embroidered on the outside of his letterman jacket

"And I am convinced that nothing can ever separate us from God's love. Neither death nor life, neither angels nor demons, neither our fears for today nor our worries about tomorrow—not even the powers of hell can separate us from God's love. No power in the sky above or in the earth below—indeed, nothing in all creation will ever be able to separate us from the love of God that is revealed in Christ Jesus our Lord."

~ *Romans 8:38–39*

Acknowledgments

I am deeply grateful to my children, Alexis and Grant, who give me life, bless me with unconditional love, and fill me with the desire to keep moving forward. To my husband, Gus, who challenges me to persevere without realizing he is building a fire of determination inside me. To my amazing parents who have been there for me every step of the way, giving me whatever I needed without question—thank you from the center of my heart.

Thank you, Dawn, for encouraging me to follow this idea and for being there every time I needed you. To Aaron, for not only believing in me, but helping me with resources, being totally honest with me, and allowing me to figure things out on my own. To Tyler, for proofing everything I have written for the Foundation, as well as ideas for this book. You and Aaron have made me laugh, when I wanted to cry, with your "Johnny" sense of humor.

I would like to express my gratitude to Debbie Rasa for making it possible to publish this book and for her support through the difficulties I endured. To Donna Wyland, who brought this book to life and made the process so incredibly smooth. God placed you both in my life at the perfect time.

To my friends who have prayed for and with me, been there without question, and been my strength on days I needed it the most.

And most of all, I give all praise and honor to God, my Father, who has shown me more love than I imagined was possible. All the glory for anything I accomplish on earth is truly His.

About the Author

Kerri LeDoux is a wife, mother, speaker, and entrepreneur committed to transforming the tragedies of her life into a message of hope and healing. After the loss of her son Johnny in 2016, Kerri founded *LiveLikeJohnny*, a nonprofit (501)(c)(3) dedicated to supporting at-risk, underserved, and often overlooked children who have the potential for personal and professional success.

In 2017, faced with the decision to return to her position in business development in the oil industry or pursue a new career, Kerri was inspired to start a new business. With support and encouragement from mentors, family, and friends—and daily guidance from God through His Word—Kerri proceeded, in faith, one step at a time, until *Heart InSouls*, *LLC* was birthed. More important than launching her company, however, Kerri provides a platform on the *Heart InSouls* web site for others to share their personal stories of standing on the promises of God.

Though small in stature, through God's strength and her unique perspective, Kerri brings a powerful voice to the message of hope and healing. She is passionate about sharing her story with audiences around the world in order to demonstrate God's ability to transform people's pain into passion and work all things together for His good as He promised He would (Romans 8:28).

Kerri resides in Jacksboro, Texas, with her husband and children. She loves spending time with her family and teaching Sunday school.

Connect with Kerri at kerri@heartinsouls.com.

At *Heart InSouls,* we seek to honor God by creating comfortable insoles that bring hope and peace to everyone who wears them. Through Scripture imprinted on the soles in their shoes, people are reminded that God loves them and has a wonderful plan for their lives.

A percentage of profits from *Heart InSouls* will be donated to the *LiveLikeJohnny* organization.

Visit www.heartinsouls.com to view our selection of Scripture-inspired insoles. Custom insoles are also available upon request.

The *LiveLikeJohnny* organization exists to continue my son's legacy of caring for kids who are often left out, ignored, or neglected. His personal mission was to do everything in his power to use his talents, skills, and abilities to change the lives of others in a positive and inspirational way.

If you have a heart like Johnny's that longs for people to know they matter, join us in our mission to provide college scholarships and mentoring opportunities to students who have a desire to discover and utilize their potential to bring good to the world through their success.

For more information, visit www.livelikejohnny.com or connect with us on Facebook, Instagram, and Twitter.

Biblical Authorities

Verses to Comfort, Encourage, and Inspire

Comfort & Peace
- "God blesses those who mourn, for they will be comforted." (Matthew 5:4)

- "He was…a man of sorrows, acquainted with deepest grief…" (Isaiah 53:3)

- "All praise be to God, the Father of our Lord Jesus Christ. God is our merciful Father and the source of all comfort. He comforts us in all our troubles so that we can comfort others. When they are troubled, we will be able to give them the same comfort God has given us." (2 Corinthians 1:3–4)

- "The LORD is close to the brokenhearted; he rescues those whose spirits are crushed." (Psalm 34:18)

- "Weeping may last through the night, but joy comes with the morning." (Psalm 30:5b)

- "For those who follow godly paths will rest in peace when they die." (Isaiah 57:2)

- "Even when I walk through the darkest valley, I will not be afraid, for you are close beside me. Your rod and your staff protect and comfort me." (Psalm 23:4)

Forgiveness & Grace

- "Let all that I am praise the LORD; may I never forget the good things he does for me. He forgives all my sins and heals all my diseases. He redeems me from death and crowns me with love and tender mercies. He fills my life with good things..." (Psalm 103:2–5)

- "For everyone has sinned; we all fall short of God's glorious standard." (Romans 3:23)

- "Most important of all, continue to show deep love for each other, for love covers a multitude of sins." (1 Peter 4:8)

- "But if we confess our sins to him, he is faithful and just to forgive us our sins and to cleanse us from all wickedness." (1 John 1:9)

- "Do not judge others, and you will not be judged. Do not condemn others, or it will all come back against you. Forgive others, and you will be forgiven." (Luke 6:37)

Hope & Healing

- "'For I know the plans I have for you,' says the LORD. 'They are plans for good and not for disaster, to give you a future and a hope.'" (Jeremiah 29:11)

- "If you openly declare that Jesus is Lord and believe in your heart that God raised him from the dead, you will be saved." (Romans 10:9)

- "Don't let your hearts be troubled. Trust in God, and trust also in me. There is more than enough room in my Father's home. If this were not so, would I have told you that I am going to prepare a place for you? When everything is ready, I will come and get you, so that you will always be with me where I am." (John 14:1–3)

- "He heals the brokenhearted and bandages their wounds." (Psalm 147:3)

- "He will wipe every tear from their eyes, and there will be no more death or sorrow or crying or pain. All these things are gone forever." (Revelation 21:4)

- "'My thoughts are nothing like your thoughts,' says the LORD. 'And my ways are far beyond anything you could imagine.'" (Isaiah 55:8)

Encouragement & Confidence
- "And we know that God causes everything to work together for the good of those who love God and are called according to his purpose for them." (Romans 8:28)

- "Keep on asking, and you will receive what you ask for. Keep on seeking, and you will find. Keep on knocking, and the door will be opened to you." (Matthew 7:7)

- "Don't love money; be satisfied with what you have. For God has said, 'I will never fail you. I will never abandon you.'" (Hebrews 13:5)

- "Take delight in the LORD, and he will give you your heart's desires." (Psalm 37:4)

- "The LORD will work out his plans for my life – for your faithful love, O LORD, endures forever." (Psalm 138:8)

- "Then Jesus said, 'Come to me, all of you who are weary and carry heavy burdens, and I will give you rest.'" (Matthew 11:28)

- "For no one is abandoned by the Lord forever. Though he brings grief, he also shows compassion because of the greatness of his unfailing love. For he does not enjoy hurting people or causing them sorrow." (Lamentations 3:31–33)

- "What shall we say about such wonderful things as these? If God is for us, who can ever be against us? Since he did not spare even his own Son but gave him up for us all—won't he also give us everything else? Who dares accuse us whom God has chosen for his own? No one—for God himself has given us right standing with himself. Who then will condemn us? No one—for Christ Jesus died for us and was raised to life for us, and he is sitting in the place of honor at God's right hand, pleading for us. Can anything ever separate us from Christ's love? Does it mean he no longer loves us if we have trouble or calamity, or are persecuted, or hungry, or destitute, or in danger, or threatened with death? No, despite all these things, overwhelming victory is ours through Christ, who loved us. And I am convinced that nothing can ever separate us from God's love. Neither death nor life, neither angels nor demons, neither our fears for today nor our worries about tomorrow— not even the powers of hell can separate us from God's love. No power in the sky above or in the earth below—indeed, nothing in all creation will ever be able to separate us from the love of God that is revealed in Christ Jesus our Lord." (Romans 8:31–39)

Faith & Trust

- "Trust in the Lord with all your heart; do not depend on your own understanding. Seek his will in all you do, and he will show you which path to take." (Proverbs 3:5–6)

- "Yes, I am the vine; you are the branches. Those who remain in me, and I in them, will produce much fruit." (John 15:5)

- "If we live, it's to honor the Lord. And if we die, it's to honor the Lord. So whether we live or die, we belong to the Lord." (Romans 14:8)

- "You light a lamp for me. The LORD, my God, lights up my darkness." (Psalm 18:28)

- "So humble yourselves under the mighty power of God, and at the right time he will lift you up in honor. Give all your worries and cares to God, for he cares about you." (1 Peter 5:6–7)

- "But the Lord is faithful; he will strengthen you and guard you from the evil one…May the Lord lead your hearts into a full understanding and expression of the love of God and the patient endurance that comes from Christ."
(2 Thessalonians 3:3, 5)

Gratitude & Thanksgiving
- "Thank you for making me so wonderfully complex! Your workmanship is marvelous…"
(Psalm 139:13–16 – selected)

- "I give you thanks, O LORD, with all my heart; I will sing your praises before the gods…I praise your name for your unfailing love and faithfulness; for your promises are backed by all the honor of your name." (Psalm 138:1–2)

- "Sing to the LORD, all you godly ones! Praise his holy name. For his anger lasts only a moment, but his favor lasts a lifetime!" (Psalm 30:4-5a)

- "Don't worry about anything; instead, pray about everything. Tell God what you need, and thank him for all he has done. Then you will experience God's peace, which exceeds anything we can understand. His peace will guard your hearts and minds as you live in Christ Jesus."
(Philippians 4:6–7)

Rejoicing & Joy

- "So you have sorrow now, but I will see you again; then you will rejoice, and no one can rob you of that joy." (John 16:22)

- "For the LORD your God is living among you. He is a mighty savior. He will take delight in you with gladness. With his love, he will calm all your fears. He will rejoice over you with joyful songs." (Zephaniah 3:17)

- "Weeping may last through the night, but joy comes with the morning." (Psalm 30:5b)

- "Always be full of joy in the Lord. I say it again—rejoice! Let everyone see that you are considerate in all you do. Remember, the Lord is coming soon." (Philippians 4:4–5)

- "Always be joyful. Never stop praying. Be thankful in all circumstances, for this is God's will for you who belong to Christ Jesus." (1 Thessalonians 5:16–18)

- "With all my heart I will praise you, O Lord my God. I will give glory to your name forever, for your love for me is very great. You have rescued me from the depths of death." (Psalm 86:12–13)

Courage & Strength

- "I trust in God, so why should I be afraid? What can mere mortals do to me?" (Psalm 56:11)

- "For I can do everything through Christ, who gives me strength." (Philippians 4:13)

- "God is our refuge and strength, always ready to help in times of trouble. So we will not fear when earthquakes come and the mountains crumble into the sea." (Psalm 46:1–2)

- "My health may fail, and my spirit may grow weak, but God remains the strength of my heart; he is mine forever." (Psalm 73:26)

- "This is my command—be strong and courageous! Do not be afraid or discouraged. For the LORD your God is with you wherever you go." (Joshua 1:9)

- "The Lord is my rock, my fortress and my deliverer; my God is my rock, in whom I take refuge, my shield and the horn of my salvation, my stronghold." (Psalm 18:2 NIV)

- "Each time he said, 'My grace is all you need. My power works best in weakness.' So now I am glad to boast about my weaknesses, so that the power of Christ can work through me." (2 Corinthians 12:9)

- "A final word: Be strong in the Lord and in his mighty power. Put on all of God's armor so that you will be able to stand firm against all strategies of the devil. For we are not fighting against flesh-and-blood enemies, but against evil rulers and authorities of the unseen world, against mighty powers in this dark world, and against evil spirits in the heavenly places." (Ephesians 6:10–12)

Resources and Notes

Scripture quotations are from *The Holy Bible*, New Living Translation (Tyndale House Foundation, 1996, 2004, 2015)

Chapter 8 Assessments List:
Spiritual Gifts and DISC Personality Assessments—available at www.uniquelyyou.org.

Clifton Strengths Questionnaire (StrengthsFinder)—visit www.gallupstrengthscenter.com.

The Enneagram Personality Test—available online at www.enneagramtest.net.

Authors quoted include the following:
Rick Warren (quotes as heard by the author on Sirius Radio 131 Family Channel)

Joyce Meyer, *Win the Battle with Power Thoughts* (Joyce Meyer Ministries, online video)

Rebekah Lyons, *You Are Free: Be Who You Already Are* (Zondervan/Harper Collins, 2017)

Oswald Chambers, *My Utmost for His Highest* (Oswald Chambers Publications Association, Ltd., 1992—original edition published in 1935 by Dodd, Mead and Company, Inc.)

The Four Stages of Grief were adapted by the author from an online source.

Order Information

To order additional copies of this book, please visit
https://redemption-press.com/encoredtp
Also available on Amazon.com and
BarnesandNoble.com or by calling toll-free
1-844-2REDEEM.

CPSIA information can be obtained
at www.ICGtesting.com
Printed in the USA
LVHW061107091218
599819LV00002B/12/P